*In Loving Memory of
Pete Valdez Sr.,
my grandfather and my friend.
His many life lessons had a profound impact on me.
Without his tough love I would not be who I am today.*

—Peter Valdez III

This book is a work of fiction. Any references to historical events, real people, or real places are used fictitiously. Other names, characters, places, and events are products of the author's imagination, and any resemblance to actual events, organizations, locales, or persons, living or dead, is entirely coincidental.

GET UP, LIL PETER. GET UP! Copyright © 2021 by Tasche Laine and Peter Valdez III
All rights reserved.

No part of this book may be reproduced in any form or by any electronic or mechanical means, including information storage and retrieval systems, without written permission from the author, except for the use of brief quotations in a book review. Thank you for your support of the author's rights.

ISBN-13: 978-1-732-12618-3 (pbk.)
ISBN-13: 978-1-732-12617-6 (eBook)

Skye Blue Press
Vancouver, WA

Get Up, Lil Peter. Get Up!

BY PETER VALDEZ AND TASCHE LAINE
ILLUSTRATED BY MEI MEI LEONARD

RING . . . RING . . . RING sounded the old-fashioned alarm clock. Lil Peter reached over and tapped off the alarm. 'I wonder who set my alarm on the first day of summer break,' he thought.

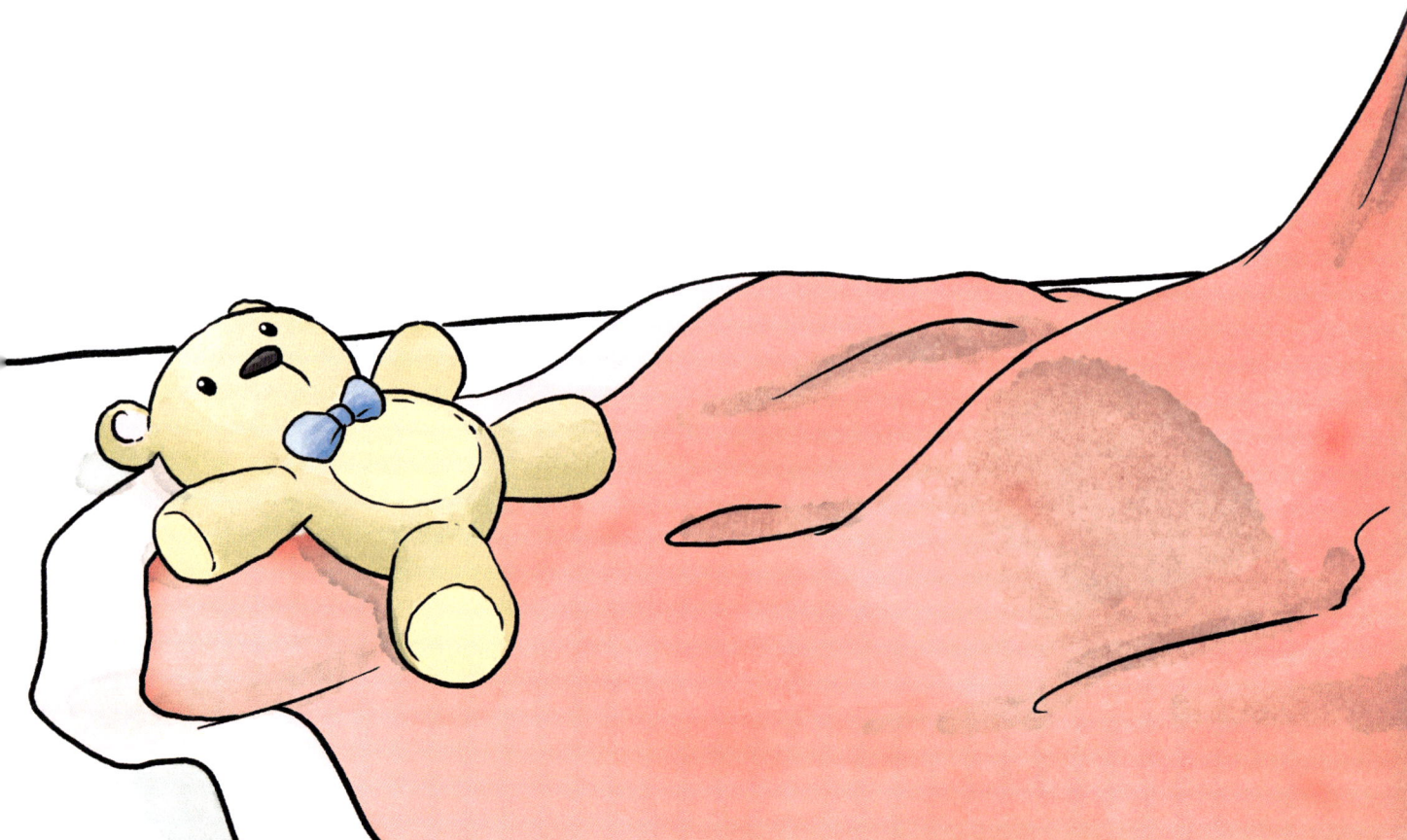

Lil Peter pulled the covers over his head to get more sleep. A familiar face popped in and said, "Get up, Lil Peter. Get up!" It was Grandpa. He spent summers with Lil Peter and his family. Grandpa must have been the one who set the alarm.

Lil Peter stretched and got out of bed. He shuffled downstairs to the aroma of sizzling bacon and French toast. Yum! Grandpa watched Lil Peter while his parents worked. It had always been just Grandpa for as long as Lil Peter could remember, for his grandma had died before he was born.

"Breakfast is ready," Grandpa said. "Grab a stool and get up, Lil Peter, get up. Let's eat before it gets cold."

Grandpa was a good friend to Lil Peter, but he didn't like computers or video games. No way! He wanted to build things and play games. Lil Peter didn't like the games because he couldn't beat Grandpa. Every time Grandpa won, Lil Peter felt frustrated.

After he won yet another game, Grandpa saw the defeated look on Lil Peter's face and said, "There is more to life than winning. Winning is easy! But losing builds character.

"Right now, you feel down. So learn from your losses. When you learn how to lose, you will figure out how to win. Lift your head up and tell your spirit to get up, Lil Peter. Get up."

One afternoon, while they played hide and seek, it was Grandpa's turn to count. Lil Peter ran to the old apple tree, filled with leaves. "He'll never find me up here," Lil Peter said to himself as he climbed up the tree. He found a good branch to sit on, determined to win this one.

It didn't take long before Lil Peter heard Grandpa's voice, "Oh were, oh where could Lil Peter be?"

Lil Peter put his hand over his mouth as he giggled, trying not to make a sound. He leaned forward to get a better view at Grandpa looking in funny places.

Lil Peter crashed through the tree branches and landed on the ground below.

"Are you hurt?" Grandpa asked, helping Lil Peter get the leaves out of his hair.

"I don't think so," Lil Peter said.

"That wasn't a very well thought out hiding spot, was it?" Grandpa said with a smirk.

"I guess not," Lil Peter said.

Grandpa reached his hand out to Lil Peter and said, "Get up, Lil Peter. Get up! It's lunchtime."

Grandpa encouraged Lil Peter to get out of the house, and to do things with his hands and mind.

One day, he helped Lil Peter build a ramp so he could jump over things with his bike. It wasn't a big ramp, but it was a lot of fun to make.

When they finished building the ramp, Grandpa lined up cans for Lil Peter to jump over. He was Lil Peter's biggest fan! He cheered him on every time Lil Peter cleared the cans, setting a new "world record."

However, not every jump was record breaking. One time, Lil Peter didn't gain enough speed to clear the last can. His bike's back tire landed on top of the can. Lil Peter lost balance and **crashed** in the grassy yard.

The crash scared and injured Lil Peter. Not badly, but it hurt enough to bring tears to his eyes.

Grandpa walked over and scanned Lil Peter for injuries. "I don't see any cuts or broken bones. I think you suffer more from that failed jump than the crash."

This made Lil Peter mad. He was hurt, and Grandpa wasn't being very sympathetic.

"Remember, failing is good!" Grandpa reminded him.

Still mad, Lil Peter wiped the tears away and said, "Good? How can it be good when I crashed?"

Grandpa smiled and said, "Failing is good. It means you tried. You succeeded in finding a way not to do something. It means you are one step closer to figuring it out! Since you are closer to achieving your goal, shouldn't you get back up on your bike? Get up, Lil Peter. Get up!"

Summer went by fast, and Grandpa and Lil Peter had many adventures together. Lil Peter failed more times than he could count. And each time he failed, Grandpa smiled and said, "Get up, Lil Peter. Get up!"

When Grandpa had to go home, Lil Peter was not happy. He sat on the porch and buried his head in his hands. He couldn't bear to watch Grandpa leave. As the tears formed, he felt a hand on his head and a familiar voice say, "Get up, Lil Peter. Get up."

Lil Peter lifted his head and wiped his eyes. In as strong a voice as he could muster, he said, "Grandpa, you have been saying that to me all summer. It used to make me mad, but now it makes me sad. Why do you always say, 'Get up, Lil Peter, get up'?"

Grandpa smiled and said, "There will be a day when I won't be there for you when you fall, when you lose, when you make poor choices, or when you hurt inside. When those times happen, I want you to hear my voice reminding you to get up. If there is one thing I want you to never forget, it is this. . . .

Just then, Lil Peter thought about every time Grandpa had said, "Get up, Lil Peter. Get up." The true meaning of his words rang clear. Grandpa's summer-long lessons ran through Lil Peter's mind.

Then Grandpa said it one more time, "Get up, Lil Peter. Get up—and give your grandpa a hug!"

Lil Peter jumped up, wrapped his arms around his grandpa, and said, "This was the best summer ever! I love you, Grandpa!"